Disconnected Thoughts

beyond modest musings

Vikiyeto Noel Jimomi

BookLeaf Publishing

India | USA | UK

Dedication

to
TOKHE
my love
my life

you are
the best thing
that ever happened to me

i get to love you
it's the best thing
that i'll ever do

Preface

Poetry has long been regarded as rhythmic, symmetric, rhymical and metered; and anyone who dares to delve into poetry using irregular prose-ish poetry may be considered unpoetic. How true! Being a musician and a lyricist, these set of poems hits that very sensitive poet's nerves in me too to edit and re-edit till they become poetry in its strict sense. However, the rebel in me wants to keep them this way, disconnected irregular but somehow intricately woven together. And this is just what I did.

Life, with all of its intricacies, remains disconnected; and all living lose their selves in the disconnection. Nevertheless, to search for that moment where one finds that single thread that weaves lives together is what poetry strives for. This was my first thought when I began writing this set of irregular poems.

Beginning with my proclamation of love for my other more significant half, this journey takes a spiritual emotional roller coaster, delving into issues such as faith, hope, afflictions, commitment, miracles, liberation, the calling, and the loss.

I believe this set will connect personally and empower, strengthen and enrich the ones who travels on the same journey.

For those who feel unconnected, may you get connected through life's greater experiences.

Vikiyeto Noel Jimomi
Kohima, Nagaland, India

Bookleaf Publication
#TheWriteAngle

Acknowledgements

GOD
for inspiration

DAD & MOM
for life

APPY, ABI, AMPY & ATO
for love

LIFE
for rich experiences

BookLeaf Publication
for the platform #TheWriteAngle

1. I Am Utterly Sure

I yearn for a statement of your love for me
But quiet are your lips;
Your lips blush readily with the essence of rubies;
They breathe life, tremble and quiver,
Yet they are silent with the words I want to hear;
Have they nothing to say? They have, I know.
Its true, words often cannot reveal
The true magic of love's potion
For words don't match
The deep density of emotion

My heart tells me your heart needs me
And you are happy, without lament
For it is not a bondage
But a devoted bond that cements.
Your smiles show the love in your soul
And my soul glows and is content
I need no words from you anymore
Of your consuming love for me;
I Am Utterly Sure.

2. Hope - I

We all are hopers.
We are creatures
who cannot stop wishing.

We are four-leaf-clover collectors.
We wish on the evening star.

We tell stories about genies
coming out of a bottle
to grant three wishes.

3. Hope - II

Hoping can break your heart.
That is why we carry
one big hope—
The secret hope
You don't even dare
to breathe.

4. Hope - III

Hope is faith
waiting
for tomorrow.

Faith requires belief,
and believing is what we do
with our minds.

Faith requires commitment,
and committing is what we do
with our wills.

But faith must also have hope,
and hoping is what we do
in our hearts.

5. "Faith-Hope Dilemma"

By Faith you Hope
for without Hope
there is no Faith

Faith dares the Soul
to the unseen beyond
in Hope

Faith makes it certain
of what is unseen
through Hope

What then,
is this
Hope?

6. beyond - i

Looking out from my window
Streets all mellow
My soul is still in the silence
As the world awaits
For some form of resilence

Yearning for the day
For us to again sway
To the sound of music
As the world watches
We dance to the acoustic

Forgoing little pleasures
Thankful to be alive
"In need" but not "in want"
Stay Home! Stay Safe!
Is that not brave?

Another time, another day
Far beyond the hills
Songs of laughter and joy
Untainted and free
We live in this hope

For life to be the same again
Will I ever see you again?
Will we ever stand
On a windswept hill
To watch the sun set?

7. beyond - ii

souls entwined, nourished
in the same womb;
beings nurtured, cultivated
by the same soul;
individuals developed, existed
in the same spectrum;
lives breathed, channelled
by the same genome.

persons survived, subsisted
yet in non-identical ways;
fates ordained, decreed
affecting each mismatched(ly);
battles struggled, won
to each their own way;
destiny determined, situated
one leaves, the other lives

absolute conception lies
beyond human perception;
they tell me –
man proposes, god disposes;
will i ever see you again?
will we ever stand
on a windswept hill
to watch the sun set?

8. Afflictions - I

(The Groan)

Sculptured out of spittle mixed with dust
Moulded in Thine Own image
Breathed with the life-giving air
Completed with a Soul that's Alive

Stricken with ornaments within
Impaired with life that grows inside
Harassed by Pain which damages
Tormented with fear of the unknown

Groaning out in agony and horror
Writhing on the ground in tears
Hoping for the healing that mayhaps will come
Longing for the touch of the Master's Hand

9. Afflictions - II

(The Plea)

this
embattled
body of mine,
battered and wrecked
at the end of my rope —
edges cut
and in tatters —
ragged and frail,
barely hanging
by a thread of hope;
and to give up
is to die;

dear SAVIOR,
please, take over —
help me survive

10. Afflictions - III

(The Healer is Here?)

Down here
in agony from my sins
hurting;
every bone broken
feels like I'm
without flesh and blood

Years pass
couldn't jump into the pond
in pain
struggling every day
not knowing
when healing would come

Authority
belongs to you and to me
its been given
through Jesus Christ
our LORD -
the healer is here

Teacher
the messiah is here now
called me
and lifted me up
i am healed
i am sick no more

The Healer was here all the time
it was me
i just could not see him
the Healer was here all the time
now i see
he made me whole again

11. Mpi Liqhi

It was not required
That You send Him
Was not the universe created
With all of its intricacies
From the words that You spoke
"Let there be" — and it was

But it was not possible
Without sending Him
My sins ran too deep
There wasn't any other way
His dear life paid that ransom
"Emptied Himself" — now I'm Free!

12. The Passover

Walking down that narrow dusty road
Trodden by many — carrying the load
Wearied, tired, torn and drawn —
Weakened by hunger and thirst;
In the horizon — beholding a sight
Of a welcoming city — bread and wine and bed
An arrow pierced Your heart — split it in two
A mourning emanating from Your soul

A vision of what was— and is — and is to come
An insight into all that I would put You through
A future where I'd add nail after nail after nail
And make You go through hell after hell after hell;
Yet not my soot You left — not a powdery grain
You cleansed it all with those tears you shed
Walking down that narrow dusty road
You passed over all my sins — redeeming me

13. The Thirteenth

They Twelve
Randomly Picked
Were they marked
In the womb
Chosen to Serve

Me
Chosen
In the womb
Called to Serve
The Thirteenth

14. God's Miracle?

sometimes
the depth of my physical suffering
is so unfathomable
that
i am amazed
at the threshold of my pain

         maybe

i am indeed
god's miracle

15. Song of Liberation?

(from afflictions to...)

hanging at rope's end
holding on to the final thread
faith willing the body to hope
mind wondering what is hope

stripped to the bones
examined by so many hands
anxious was the wait
hoping in faith

miracles they do happen
foretold before i sojourned
jewels gone — to trouble no more
happiness — knows no bounds

16. the call, the response

the ground is wet, the grass is cold
the air is moist, chills — up my spine

hearts are broken, lives are lost
in the darkness, souls are wailing

is there no one, who will go down
to lift them up, from this misery

here i am lord! send me o lord
i go down, i bring them home

17. a worshipper's call

(to serve, not to be served)

down in the valley, souls gather
lost, in pain...chained down
by their own sins

been called out by God, to reach out
to those lost souls
crying out in agony

can you shout out?
can you raise a hand?

i am here O Lord
send me down O Lord
to the dying souls
bring them to you

there'll be rejoicing, when even one
of these precious
is brought back to Him

great is your reward - in heaven
and on the earth
your purpose be fulfilled

18. the loss - i

each life
a mural on the wall;
every happening
painted on our tapestry;
weaving through
the laughter and tears;
memories — our souvenirs

and suddenly,
you know it's time,
to start something new;
and trust
the magic of beginnings

19. the loss - ii

and...

and as we bid farewell,
to loved ones who journey before us,
our hearts eternally whisper,
aching for the timbre of their voice

and when our lives are but memories,
long lost like the breath of wind,
we shall find each other once again,
consoled by the tears of our long embrace

and beauty, though piercing,
will not leave us undone,
for our love will bind us together,
and we shall always know that we are truly one

20. the loss - iii

and suddenly
it dawned on me tonight
that you are really gone
never to come back again

and even memories
are like embers
slowly fading away
into the night

21. The Differently Different

every sunset
with its different colors
reminds me
that every life
is differently different

if only
everyone
would take time
to recognize
these differently different

then
mayhaps
this world would become
a better place for
these differently different

www.ingramcontent.com/pod-product-compliance
Lightning Source LLC
La Vergne TN
LVHW021329200726
843509LV00014B/2463